MINESTA'S VISION

A Centenary Collection of Grace Cooke's Writings

With illustrations by Cloda Whyte

THE WHITE EAGLE PUBLISHING TRUST
NEW LANDS · LISS · HAMPSHIRE · ENGLAND

First published June 1992

© Text copyright, The White Eagle Publishing Trust, 1992
Illustrations © Cloda Whyte, 1992

British Library Cataloguing-in-Publication Data
A catalogue record for this book is available from the British Library

ISBN 0-85487-089-X

Set in 11 on 13pt and 12 on 15pt Galliard,
and printed in Great Britain by Acme Printing Co. Ltd., Portsmouth, Hampshire

CONTENTS

BIBLIOGRAPHICAL NOTE

All the books which contain autobiographical chapters by 'Minesta' (Grace Cooke) and which are quoted in the text of the present one are out of print, as stated in the introduction, opposite. A third volume with autobiographical material, but also out of print, is PLUMED SERPENT(Rider & Co., 1942). The only other extracts from them which are at present available are those reproduced in THE STORY OF THE WHITE EAGLE LODGE (White Eagle Publishing Trust, 1986), which also contains a full bibliography of books of, or associated with, White Eagle's teaching, up to that date.Ivan Cooke's THE WHITE BROTHERHOOD (1939), mentioned on p. 32, is also out of print; and so, at the time of the present book going to press, is THE RETURN OF ARTHUR CONAN DOYLE (1956). All other books mentioned in the text are still available and published by The White Eagle Publishing Trust, except THE GOLDEN KEY (Psychic Press, 1988). A full list of Minesta's books currently in print and those containing White Eagle's teaching is available from the publishers.

INTRODUCTION

THE OCCASION for this little book is a birthday celebration—perhaps rather an unorthodox birthday celebration, as the anniversary it marks is the centenary of the leader and co-founder of the White Eagle Lodge, now in the world of spirit. This collection of unpublished or long-out-of-print writings by Grace Cooke is, in form, a companion volume to the little book BRIGHT NEW YEAR, a miscellany of Ivan Cooke's writings published in tribute in 1989. This present book of Grace Cooke's writings has though a larger purpose than a warm personal tribute or even a collection of spiritual writings. As the title suggests the theme running through the book is that of vision. We hope within the limited bounds of the following pages to share a wider picture than is perhaps generally known of the vision held by Grace Cooke (or Minesta—this was the name given to her by her teacher and guide in spirit, White Eagle) into the world of light. And this theme of vision gives a more than personal perspective to the book; we are seeing glimpses of that illumined thread of greater guidance which shaped her life, but which came for a purpose beyond her own. Grace Cooke herself said towards the end of her physical life that if a biography of her was ever written the purpose should be to make real the wonderful pattern of guidance which was demonstrated through the life of a very human being.

This book however is not in any way a biography, even though a very few personal details have been sketched in to give a background to several of the passages of her own writing which are collected here. In reading the extracts it may be helpful to remember too that for much of her life she was giving up her own voice, as it were, to enable White Eagle to speak his message. Although she had a natural Geminian enjoyment of communication, her own writing took second place. She probably filled far more pages in writing personal letters in the course of her spiritual work, than she did in writing articles, or books. There is no complete picture of her life here, but we hope that this book nonetheless conveys a sweet and courageous personality, through whose life the inspiration of new vision was felt by so many.

Some of the writing is taken from short, early books, out of print for many years: THE OPEN DOOR (1946); and THE SHINING PRESENCE (1946), subsequently re-issued in part as THE ILLUMINED ONES. Much of the rest of the writing is taken from the journal *Angelus*, the journal of the White Eagle Lodge between 1936 and 1952, and of course from the present magazine *Stella Polaris*. A few of the passages are from unpublished talks given either in a public service or at special meetings for the inner brotherhood work within the White Eagle Lodge.

In the passage at the end of this book, Ylana Hayward describes the impression received in meditation of Minesta's home and place of work in the spirit life, and records that Minesta seemed 'very anxious not to be thought of as someone special'. Because many of the passages are examples of spiritual vision we have deliberately included some personal detail, particularly in the first chapter, which shows just a little of the ordinary human experience in the midst of which these visions, insights and convictions flowered. Although she was so open to the joy of the spiritual world, her life had its own share of pain; and her own childhood experiences, for instance, gave her enormous sympathy with those who were bereaved. By way of a little personal detail, I myself recall, as a boy, her scrupulousness in not wanting a grandmother's generosity to remove a teenager's sense of financial independence—an independence which I know that she herself had to earn with some struggle at a similar age. I note this just as a pointer to the fact that Minesta's vision was born in the ploughed soil of human experience we all share, and not—as she herself would so much wish to disclaim—in the life of a 'cardboard saint'.

For those to whom this book may be a first contact with Grace Cooke's life and work a brief note may be helpful about names: the name 'Minesta' was given to her by White Eagle and she felt it referred to a South American Indian life she described in her book THE ILLUMINED ONES, where the link between her and White Eagle was that of father and daughter. This name became very widely used by those close to her or much involved in White Eagle's work. Earlier, however, White Eagle had also given her the familiar and affectionate name 'Bright Eyes'—not only of course because as a young woman her eyes were particularly vivacious and alight, but denoting in a human way the ability of those eyes to open to a vision beyond the horizon of the material world.

We have said that this book cannot give a full picture of Minesta's work, or even of Minesta herself; we hope though that through her own words the reader will feel drawn close to some aspects of her personality: a gentle mother, comforter to many, who knew a great warmth of human love; a sensitive, but practical mystic, who could turn with alarming swiftness from inner vision to a need for 'getting down to it'; in spite of the gentleness of her vision a tireless witness, even a fighter, for the reality of the spiritual world. Writing in 1992 we are aware of the huge change of awareness that has truly taken place in the acceptance of the reality of a spiritual life which embraces the physical. For Minesta, part of the 'golden thread' running through her life was the work of breaking through the crust of a whole habit of living and thinking which excluded awareness of the inner worlds. In the last months of her life we recall her saying, with typical down-to-earthness, as she thought of the pattern in her life's work: 'I feel from White Eagle that we have got in the thin end of the wedge!'—the wedge in the door which opens to a state of life illumined by the light of the spirit, the true heritage of all people. May this modest record of her life inspire us all to continue her work with equal integrity, gentleness, and courage.

AJH
May 1992

CHAPTER ONE

Moments of Autobiography from Early Years

WE BEGIN with Minesta's childhood. Grace Evelyn Imison was born as the ninth child of a large family, on 9th June 1892. Grace's own memory of her mother was of a woman who looked after her youngest daughter devotedly, even with the size of the family; and perhaps all the more so as there was a gap of some years between Grace and her brothers and sisters. In 1889, however, Emma Imison died, leaving a devastated family and her youngest child only seven years old. In order to understand the first autobiographical passage below, this child's own account in later life of her mother's passing, we need both to think and feel back to the different atmosphere of the last years of the last century. In a large family stricken by grief, Grace would have found herself surrounded by the heaviness of adult emotion and all the sombre trappings that were thought appropriate to a family bereavement. As we understand it, what had happened was not straightforwardly explained to the young child—probably from the motive of protecting her— but at the same time she would have been acutely sensitive to the emotional atmosphere in the family house, as well as being aware, with a child's practicality, of her mother's passing. Against this background there was the young Grace's intense, childish conviction of spiritual reality and her certainty that her mother had only changed her outward form. Surrounded by the atmosphere of hushed grief, which as a child she could neither fully understand nor absorb, Grace clung to her 'secret'; her inner knowledge that in no way could her mother 'die'. In the passage below we can see the young girl's unshakeable conviction, but also her emotional vulnerability to suggestions from the adult world. We believe too that that physical loss and early turning of her love towards a mother in the world of spirit helped focus the vision of her soul on the inner world of light, when all the mental habits with which she would have been surrounded as she grew up might otherwise have dimmed this conviction.

✍ My mother died when I—the youngest member of a family of nine—was seven years old. The veiled angel of death visited our home and drew my mother within the dark folds of her robe, and she was borne away on the shining wings of death to another home. So I thought and believed; but people around me spoke in whispers about the motherless little girl and said how sad a loss it was for one so young. These remarks did not penetrate my understanding. In my heart and in the little mental world in which I lived, I knew my mother was not dead; for me that seemed impossible. I imagined she had been transported to a more beautiful home; she was now living with angels in heaven, but not dead—of course not.

In my mind death had become something associated with the earth—with a big hole in the ground; with sickly-smelling white flowers and much whispering, melancholy and mystery; and with people dressed in black clothes, the women wearing voluminous dark veils hanging over their faces and drooping down their backs. Surely mother could not be linked up with any of these ugly things? Somewhere she was still happy, smiling, singing. I knew that a light dwelt inside her body, shining through it now as a light might shine out through the windows of a house. I was sure that this was so, for I had seen her myself on several occasions since I had been told she was dead. Once a foolish whispering scared voice asked me if it were true that my mother was dead. I looked at my questioner and turned away with a quivering lip, without saying a word.

That some change had taken place I fully admitted. My mother was not now quite as I had known her during the tender years of childhood's memory—this I recognized; but that she was well and happy and very much alive I hadn't a shadow of a doubt. Later in life I saw a tombstone which bore the inscription: 'To commemorate the transition of...' In this manner I thought of the talked-of death of my mother. She was changed somewhat because she had become more radiant; and she now spent a lot of time in a beautiful place where there were angels, but this did not make her forget about me, her baby girl. Indeed I saw her frequently, sitting by the fireside in her own low chair, more especially on Sunday evenings, just as she used to sit when she joined in the hymns we had loved to sing with her.

I remember going into the drawing room after tea one day. My entry seemed to bring a hush over the assembled members of the family. Somewhat startled by the oddness of the silence, I noticed one of my older sisters sitting in my mother's accustomed chair. She seemed asleep, but my father said: 'Go and say goodnight to your sister "B", and kiss her nicely.' Quite naturally I went up to kiss her, and found myself enfolded in a loving embrace and tenderly kissed. Not a word was spoken but I knew then that it was my mother's love and kiss which made my heart leap. No, of course mother was not dead! She was here in our midst now: she had kissed and embraced me as she had done on many occasions. She had drawn very close to my sister so that she might do so. She would never die.

In the months after her mother's passing the whole family became interested in the investigation of Spiritualism, and two of her elder sisters eventually found they possessed some considerable degree of psychic gift. For Grace herself her family's contact with Spiritualism seems to have brought confirmation of her own inner conviction and support for her secret awareness. She continues the story in her own words in the first chapter of her book THE SHINING PRESENCE.

✎ About this time my father made some investigations into psychic communion between the two states of life; and, through the instrumentality of Mrs Annie Boddington, became convinced of both the possibility and the truth of such communion. To this gifted woman my family and I owe much. She opened the door which led me, when very young, into a new world. I remember vividly her first talk to me about little children who passed into fairyland when they died. She strengthened my own conclusions concerning that other world, more beautiful than this, into which people passed. Her gifts of spiritual vision, so unselfishly devoted to the cause of truth, were the means of setting me on a path of similar service. From then onwards communion with our loved one became an accepted and beautiful truth to us all.

I have never tried to induce my own psychic powers, because from the age of seven it became normal for me to see spirit people and to hear their conversation. I could at will slip through the 'crack' between this world and the next for as long as I wanted to, to enter a world which some might call 'all imagination'. Apart from this, all kinds of friendly spirit people often came to me in my room at night, and particularly North American Indians. I loved these kindly folk who, I thought, took care of me when I slept.

When about twelve I had my first experience of giving correct evidence of the life after death. I was taken to visit a sick woman—a total stranger; I felt very sorry for her because she was so sad and ill. I could not keep my eyes from her, and as I was gazing, I noticed that the wall and a screen immediately behind her faded from sight, and a little girl appeared holding a doll in her arms. I suppose other people in the room noticed my fascinated gaze, for a voice broke across my reverie asking me what I was 'seeing'. I described the exact appearance of the little girl and repeated what she said to me. She gave her name and said she had come to see her darling mother who was ill and who feared she would never again see her own home and her husband (the child's father). Little Lilian told her mother that she would get perfectly well and would return to South Africa. Then the scene changed—I can remember it clearly. Now I was looking at a picture of a substantial veldt homestead in a charmingly laid-out garden, and on the verandah of the house a man was sitting, smoking a pipe.

My hostess was astounded. She said that the child was her little girl who had died three years before; the scene was an accurate description of her South African home; the man was her husband, sitting, as was his practice in the cool of the evening, smoking his corncob pipe. According to South African time it would now be evening—the hour when he would relax and rest. Joy overcame the suffering woman, for proof had been given that not only was her so-called 'dead' child still living, but that she was happy and well. By bringing her favourite doll, Lilian had shown her mother how natural was the life beyond and how little she was changed. Moreover a power which could overcome time and space had been demonstrated, for the child had not only come herself, but a living picture of her daddy from the other side of the world had been given.

I was amazed when I realized what my vision had meant to another. It was beautiful to see such joy and happiness shine from the sick woman's face. A few days before she had believed her illness to be incurable and had even prepared her mind for death. But now her little child had from the other world assured her mother that she would completely recover and return to her husband and her home. Within five months the prediction was fulfilled.

As is so much more recognized now, for many children there is still some openness of vision or intuitive awareness of the spiritual home from which they have come—their awareness is not wholly limited to the five physical senses and earthly brain, which can form the settled and maybe heavy clothing of physical incarnation. For Grace as a child, whom she herself describes as 'rather a lonely little girl', the passage between the outer everyday, and the inner, worlds seems to have been entirely natural and the boundary blurred; this was especially so close to the time of sleeping and waking. In another early book, THE OPEN DOOR, she speaks of her first awareness of White Eagle, the unknown friend who kept in her awareness the joy and beauty of a wider world. It must be said too that although from her eighth year Grace entered the Spiritualist Lyceum Sunday school, in no way was any attempt made in the following years deliberately to develop a child's psychic faculties—something which she herself in later life would also have strongly discouraged. What we are given in the following passage is a picture of the natural extension of childish vision, even if this extension was developed to an unusual degree.

✍ My friend White Eagle was a fairly constant visitor when I was a child. Usually he came at night, or sometimes in the morning when I awoke he used to be waiting. Often he was alone, but occasionally he brought spirit children with him, or other friends whom he wanted me to know. In this manner I became familiar with children of other races, so that in time it did not seem strange that black, brown, yellow or red skinned children should play with a little white child who was on the whole rather a lonely little girl.

To that child White Eagle became dear and familiar. He wasn't like anyone else of my acquaintance—the people around me, I mean; he wasn't dressed like them but reminded me more of one of the disciples whose pictures I had seen in our old family Bible, for he wore a white robe underneath a cloak of soft blue lined with amethyst, with a crown of soft feathers about his head. In some way his dress was like that of an American Indian, but not entirely, with the exception of his high feathered headdress. On closer examination he could have been taken for some ancient mythical, mystical and knight-like character, bearing himself with an air of nobility as well as simplicity. He himself and even his clothing seemed to emit a gentle radiance, which alone removed him from the level of an ordinary man, or of the Red Indians of which I had read in storybooks. Between the two, neither wholly Red Indian nor wholly heavenly and angelic, he might have stepped out of some world of the past. Of course, I didn't realize or perplex myself with these matters at the time, but accepting him as he was, felt a deep and genuine love for him, for the melody of his voice and the way his kind eyes twinkled and danced when he was telling a story or organizing some game among the children. We seemed to be all members of a group met in a charming garden in which we played and in which were velvety green lawns and many clumps of bushes like rhododendron and lilac in profuse bloom. Did we want to rest after our games, swings and hammocks for the young people were slung from the branches of the trees.

As has been said, I didn't ask myself many questions about these wonders, but took them for granted. We used to play with large balls, some nearly as big as a football, others about the size of a tennis ball and full of colour and light, so that they seemed not unlike large soap bubbles. So airy were they that they used to bounce as well as float about and would fly a long way in the direction we wanted when impelled by our hands. There were streams of water in this garden, too, and lakes upon which swans and ducks swam. On the latter were small boats, often shaped like large swans, in which our bigger playfellows used to take two or three children. Together we would glide over the lake to its boundaries or to an island in its centre; often pausing to laugh and play and talk, or to watch the insect life in the water, the bird life in the trees and bushes, and also little people like fairy people visible to us amongst the flowers that carpeted the ground beneath the trees. Many lovely games have I enjoyed in this wonderland.

At such times I never thought of how I got there. It was sufficient to know when I fell asleep that when I woke White Eagle would be standing by my bedside: and the familiar walls of my room would gradually melt away and I would find myself in the spirit garden amongst the other children, my heart and soul in the fun of the game which White Eagle or some other visitor had taught us to play in my fairyland—which is to me a world of lightness, beauty and enthralling happiness.

In this passage we see the beginning of a relationship which was not to come into full flower until over twenty years later when this loving figure, to whom Grace did not in childhood days even attach the name 'White Eagle', first spoke through her human instrumentality. We can perhaps marvel at the unperturbed patience and planning of those in the world of light. Many phases of life's experiences lay ahead, before Minesta's true work for White Eagle unobtrusively began.

It may be helpful to give the briefest picture of the open-eyed and unconsciously gifted child, whose connecting line of light with the inner world was so strong. She was brought up in a kindly-intentioned, but emphatically strict way by her elder sisters, whose attempts to discipline the vivacity of the youngest member of the family were firm, but by no means always successful—a family picture of her was of a champagne bottle with a cork which kept on popping up! Although she was part of a large and interactive family and herself spoke of warm memories of family games and dances in which many of her brothers and sisters were involved, there is also a theme of loneliness and a feeling of being emotionally misunderstood running through her youthful experiences. Her father remarried and Grace felt her stepmother's behaviour towards her as so unjust that eventually she was taken to live with one of her elder sisters. She left school at fourteen and had a secretarial training with a London firm, eventually working for Spicers the papermakers. The impression from her adolescent years is of circumstances which brought a strong discipline and also the need to fend for herself emotionally—in spite of her shyness to stand up for the truth of her own feelings.

In her teens Minesta often found herself giving evidential communication or vision from the other side of life and at the age of twenty-one she gave her first public lecture and demonstration of clairvoyance from a Spiritualist platform. Many years of work followed within the Spiritualist movement; her work on the public platform being done in conjunction with bringing up her own family. It was hard work, often in ungenerous and even harsh conditions. Grace herself noted: 'At weekends I journeyed north, south, east and west, addressing audiences of varying sizes, sceptical and otherwise. Frequently during the week some afternoon or evening meeting called me away from home and children. Here the loyalty and helpfulness of my family proved a great asset to me. We shared the spiritual work, as it were; we all pulled together.' In her late twenties Minesta, together with her husband, Ivan Cooke, received strong intuition and guidance, that a new phase of life lay ahead for her—a phase which was in itself to be a preparation for her real future work. This new phase was a move to Western Australia. It was a great upheaval of her home and not undertaken without deep inner searching, as she herself makes clear in her account of the family's journey to a new life in Australia.

✍ The decision to go to Australia was a test and no easy one. I loved England, my home and all my people. I shrank from the unknown future; this statement may seem contradictory, since many of my experiences in connection with spiritual work have been explorations into the unknown, but never before had I been called upon to break up my home and sever myself from all but my immediate family.

After weeks of preparation we embarked at Tilbury for our unknown destination in what I saw as the wilds of the Australian bush. I had determined, once the decision had been made, that I would go straight forward without so much as a backward glance. Even on the ship I found myself involuntarily looking towards the bows. This attitude of mind became natural. Some inner purpose deeper and more insistent than any earthly prospect called and would not be denied.

The journey was not without its incidents and amongst other experiences I was taken ill after getting a 'touch of the sun' at Port Said. The temperature of the ship's hospital was too torrid to be endured. I lay on deck desperately ill; and during a breathless tropical night, while the ship throbbed her way down the Red Sea, I called upon and faced the power of the Infinite. The sky was a heavy indigo canopy hung with myriads of tiny lights. I had never before seen so many stars of such brilliance. In my fever and weakness I remember making a supreme effort. I *willed* that I should overcome the dreadful sickness which had sapped my strength and brought death so very near. I felt the power and reality of God draw very close ... and then suddenly the crisis passed and I knew for certain that my present life would continue until I had fulfilled the mission which had been given me. The rest of our voyage was happy and uneventful.

One bright July morning, when white billowy clouds sailed across the deep blue sky—a sky typical of Australia—we steamed into Fremantle Harbour, Western Australia. Our first task was to find a suitable home away in 'bushland'. This was not easy and six or eight weeks were spent in the search. In the meantime we met with great kindness and hospitality in the seaside resort called Cottesloe Beach—about eight miles from Perth. The memory of walks along the white silver sands by the side of the deep blue ocean and the sparkling foam of the great rollers breaking upon the seashore will never be lost.

At last our search was rewarded and we moved to a farm of three hundred and fifty acres situated about eighty miles from Perth and five miles from the nearest township, Harvey.

When we arrived at our new home I felt somewhat dismayed. It seemed almost terrifyingly lonely, for having lived all my life in London the silence and expanse of this 'never-never' land engulfed and threatened to overwhelm me. The house might almost be described as a shed or humpy, built of rough-hewn timber and roofed with corrugated iron, the supporting rafters making a fine run for mice and (as we discovered subsequently) for sizeable rats. However, it was roomy and gave promise of being developed into an attractive home.

One had to get familiar with a smoky kitchen range; when in a good mood and the logs of wood (the only available fuel) dry, it very quickly got roasting hot and baked bread, cakes and pastry beautifully, giving the food a delicious flavour which can only be obtained by cooking with wood fuel.

We had no water laid on—another shock! As water had to be drawn from a soak a hundred yards distant and carried to the house, economy became the order of the day. This soak was a large square hole about twenty feet deep and four or five feet square, from which the water had to be drawn up by a hand bucket. Its contents seemed not over-appetizing at first, and many were the little wriggling creatures which swam in it, but I was assured by someone who was accustomed to bush life that it was pure and wholesome. We soon got used to its flavour and even welcomed it in hot weather, and as the summer wore on, husbanded our remaining stock—by now even less appetizing— with zealous care.

A delightful feature of our new home was a border of tall arum lilies which grew on both sides of the path up to the front verandah. I remember that *Gloire de Dijon* roses, mixed with pink ivy geraniums and asparagus fern, climbed over and shaded the front verandah.

The early morning song of the magpies I shall never forget. Although I had been told that Australia was a land of songless birds and scentless flowers, I had never before heard such pure melody as from this bird chorus. As for the flowers, the perfume of our roses and lilies bore testimony to the error of such a statement.

Life in the Australian bush has its hardships, but it also has much charm. I can look back upon this period with tender and happy memories. I felt that we became pioneers on the three planes of being—physical, mental and spiritual. Any doubts of the guidance which had brought us across twelve thousand miles of ocean to settle in these natural surroundings were soon dispelled. The two children throve on the sweet-scented sunlit air and the perfect freedom of their life. The great expanse of bush held no terrors for them. They grew accustomed to seeing wallabies and sometimes 'boomer' kangaroos leaping across our paddocks, and to hearing the 'thud-thud' of their great hind feet as they landed on the earth after each jump. Snakes were plentiful, as were centipedes and tarantula spiders and large 'bull' ants. Flies at certain seasons were innumerable and I could write of many encounters with these and other small pests. The bush, in spite of its solemn loneliness and its expanse, is not without a certain liveliness at times.

A raging bush fire can be a terrifying experience. The intense heat and the dense smoke render one almost incapable of action. I recall one occasion on which we seemed to be surrounded by fires on all sides. They crept towards our little wooden house, already baking under the summer sun. A stray spark would have been sufficient to set the whole building ablaze and reduce it to ashes within half an hour. We were ready for it; with wet towels over our mouths, the four of us beat at the creeping flames with branches torn from the eucalyptus trees and eventually extinguished the fire, but not before it had reached within a few yards of the house. Yes, life in the bush has its exciting moments, especially in the summer months....

We left Western Australia in October, 1923, and I knew as we walked in the peaceful garden for the last time that we were saying goodbye to a life of tranquil happiness. Henceforth I felt that a path of wider service would open before me, and this proved to be true.

On her return from Australia a quieter, domestic period followed for a few years before she was drawn again more fully into arduous public work. At the same time she wrote, 'During what might be described as a time of quiescence, and whilst occupied in domestic work, I would receive from time to time a visit from a denizen of the other world'. The result of one such contact made in the sanctuary of her own home led to the transmitting of the descriptive messages that form the basis of the book THE GOLDEN KEY. It was whilst staying in Switzerland, engaged in this work, that an apparently chance contact led to another new phase in Minesta's life—the setting up of a home for spiritual work at Burstow Manor in Sussex. The story of Burstow, and the link both with Arthur Conan Doyle and with the Polaire Brotherhood in France, has been told in THE RETURN OF ARTHUR CONAN DOYLE and THE STORY OF THE WHITE EAGLE LODGE; these years opened the way for the eventual founding of the Lodge in 1936.

CHAPTER TWO

Skye and Iona

IN THE YEARS following the founding of the Lodge in 1936 Minesta and her family frequently took their holiday in the west of Scotland. A stay on the island of Iona was a revelation for both Minesta and 'Brother Faithful' (Ivan Cooke). Many readers who have made the same journey from Oban, across Mull (in those days in a bone-shaking bus), and arrived at Fionnphort to see Iona spread out before them, like a haven of gentleness in the wild purity of the west of Scotland, will understand how Minesta could feel that she had found somewhere where her spirit was returning home. Some years later she wrote in the magazine *Angelus*:

✍ Last evening's mail brought a letter from the Editor of *Angelus* asking me for a contribution to the Christmas issue of *Angelus*, and so this morning I sit on the white sandy shore and look out across a turquoise sea bathed in sunlight, which is the Sound of Iona, to the rose-hued foreground and purple hills of Mull beyond. As I write, I sense the spiritual magic of this place, and see revealed the etheric impression left by the simple,

tranquil and holy lives of the gentle brethren who lived here centuries, aye, even ages gone by. Perhaps even Iona's present generation has inherited some serenity of spirit, which comes with the joy of a life lived within the arms of Mother Nature. The September air is full of the scents of grasses and flowers.

As I walk along the rough island roads which run between the farms and hills and listen to the lowing of the cattle and the song of the birds, the spirit of peace and the love of life is wafted on the soft wind, which to me has a purifying effect upon the soul. I feel I have slipped off the heavy burden of strain from my shoulders, and am striding along life's high road, joyous and carefree.

Ivan Cooke was equally drawn to Iona and it was here that he developed the gift for painting which became a life-long creative activity.

All part of the natural beauty of the surroundings for Minesta was the inner blessing which she sensed Iona held. She felt this was a heritage, not only from St Columba's settlement on the island, but from even earlier times, as she wrote in 1971 in her book THE LIGHT IN BRITAIN.

With the outbreak of the second world war the spiritual contact she had made on Iona, and the closeness she had felt to the whole natural world in the west of Scotland, helped to give her courage as she sustained the work of the White Eagle Lodge through the war years. The following article, describing an opening of her vision to the inner worlds whilst staying on the island of Skye, shows how deeply she felt the need to keep alive the vision of the spiritual life unseen behind the otherwise all-embroiling physical conflict and tragedy. For her too, as for everyone caught up in the outbreak of war, there were times when 'the heavens seemed as brass', yet White Eagle's strong assurance of a greater reality, glimpsed perhaps more easily on the blessed isle of Iona, carried her and the work of the Lodge through the extremely rough waters of those years into peace.

✍ There is a sentence which stands out clearly in my mind just now; it was written to me by a man overcome by grief through the loss of his only son—a boy aged fifteen years. He wrote 'Until I received your message from my boy in spirit, *it seemed as though the heavens were as brass.*' This might apply to many today, who have been shocked and disillusioned by the sudden announcement of war.

With all the activity of warfare going on in the material world, the beauty of the spirit world, and its gentle loving guides and companions, seems to have receded far into the background of our consciousness, and 'the heavens have seemed as brass'.

On the wall in White Eagle's sanctuary at the Lodge, there hangs a pastel drawing of purple mountains encompassing a lake of deep blue, on the shores of which sits the shadowy outline of an American Indian. The scene and his posture suggests profound stillness and deep meditation as he gazes outward towards the purple range of mountains. The mystical conception of the picture, which was drawn under the inspiration of White Eagle himself, conveys a deep impression that just behind the misty veil of purple light which rests over the mountains, is a temple of the cosmic Brotherhood, from which is being sent forth to earth's humanity, wisdom, love and power. The nearness of the unseen presence is clearly conveyed in this picture of White Eagle's spirit home.

It has called to mind a holiday spent this year in the Western Isles of Scotland, where we lingered for a week in the sunny and misty Isle of Skye. Some islanders' conception of heaven is a beautified Isle of Skye; and truly, a visit to this enchanting and enchanted island convinces the visitor of the heavenly charm of the place. It was whilst rambling over the heather-clad hills, by the side of a deep blue sea-loch, canopied by one of the bluest skies I have ever seen, that the fairylike atmosphere of the island dawned upon my inner and outer consciousness. Clairvoyantly I penetrated behind the land and seascape of earthly beauty, and saw the harmony and loveliness of the spirit world which interpenetrated its material counterpart. What was invisible to mortal vision, was a world which touched my spirit; it was like fairy hands playing the harp within my soul, and as the fairy music that I could hear rose and fell in sweet cadence, my eyes saw the delicacy and beauty of that other world which lay just behind the veil of earthly vision. I saw the countless fairy folk, apparently playing in the purple heather and soft bracken. I saw the gracious forms of the sylphs, or air spirits, sweeping the sky and directing the air currents; and I saw the sea sprites playing with the white foam as the water lapped the beach beneath the rocky promontory on which I sat. The real world, God's world, was revealing itself to my spirit.

There are many tales told by the Islanders about the fairy folk and their kindly ministry to needy humankind, but it has been said by some authors that such tales are second-hand, and that there is no proof that anyone has actually had an experience with fairy folk. Be that as it may, the memory of the fairy pipes which I heard, played by fairy hands, will live with me through the remaining years of my present incarnation. It was no fantasy, but real pipe music which I heard on that lonely spot on the Isle of Skye. It was not until afterwards that I happened to hear that it was near this spot that the first Macrimon (the Macrimons were the most famous of all pipers) heard the fairy music and was given a silver chanter by the fairies, and with it the great gift of piping. What, I wonder, is the real origin of this legend?

My recent experiences on Skye, and later, on the Isle of Iona, have opened a soul vision into the world beyond which I pray may never again be dimmed. A few days ago, since the fears and horrors of war engulfed our brethren at home and abroad, I wandered across a heather-clad common on the south of England, and entering a natural 'cathedral' built of stalwart pines, I prayed for a deeper vision into the future days of humanity. And as I waited in the stillness, the voice spoke, saying 'War is no more. It is finished. The angels are singing: "Peace comes on earth, and goodwill *shall be* among all men".' And I knew in my soul that the voice spoke truly. The peace and brotherhood which lies behind the mist of materialism now hanging over the earth, will, most surely, come into manifestation on earth. The presence of the unseen is with us now, as always; God has given His angels charge over the earth and her children. The silent, invisible helpers wait at the door between earth and heaven. The handle is on the earth side of life, and the power which will turn the handle and open the door is love, the spirit of Christ in everyman. In the same way as my vision revealed the presence of the fairy folk on the Isle of Skye, so today I see the great company of radiant souls of men and women who have passed into the spirit world, and now return to the earth, to guide and inspire those whom they still love, towards the life of brotherhood. The dawn of this day of brotherhood awaits the coming of a clearer understanding to man of the real values, of the spiritual truths, which lie within the unseen Kingdom of Christ.

We end this section with a description of the end of another, later, visit to Iona, after the years of war were past.

✍ During that time we had the joy of seeing Iona often illumined by sunlight which brought out in the seas all the lovely jewelled lights of deep ultramarine and sapphire blue, inter-threaded with light emerald green, and splashed here and there with violet and amethyst. It is impossible for the most prosaic individual not to 'feel' the magic on the Isle of Iona. The long tiring journey to this holy spot 'in the Sun' is thus well worth the effort, for one returns to the workaday world filled with renewed life and fresh vision. I can so vividly re-live the minutes when we moved away from the grey and green marbled rocks and the white sands of Iona, which had witnessed in ages past so many dedicated, uplifted lives, and also the martyrdom of many of the sainted ones who had died there for their faith. So we turned our faces towards the great pink-tinged rocks of Mull, and the ferry took us across the Sound of Iona on our journey back to the mainland. As we went I felt *their* presence—their whispered farewells and their blessing, and their promise that we should in the days to come return to this most ancient land.

We journeyed on by bus over the very rough roads across Mull.

CHAPTER THREE

Angels and Divine Mother

IN READING through the talks which Minesta gave in the course of the Lodge work, we have been struck by how often she spoke of the angelic presence at a service, or meeting. She was especially led to help those who under White Eagle's influence were drawn to open their own understanding and feeling to the angelic presence which attends any dedicated act of healing, or of worship. She followed White Eagle's prompting, too, in continually bearing witness to the angelic life behind nature. She also felt that lightness of spirit was necessary to make this contact. For instance, once during a harvest festival service she began her talk with the following words, which give a feeling that she almost wanted everyone to dance.

✍ It was lovely to hear that little hymn sung by you all. It brought such a bright vibration into this service. It seems that it is this simplicity that the spirit strives for. The spirit does not really like to be, it cannot be, weighed down by a lot of heaviness. It does not like ponderous things. It likes the gay, sincere happy things.

I feel very strongly impressed upon this day of thanksgiving for the harvest to speak to you about the angels, because we are so close to the day of St Michael and All Angels. At this time I can assure you that there is a very powerful contact between the angelic world and the earth plane. And I would remind you also what a big part angels play in the work of producing the rich harvest from the earth. It always seems to me a deep truth that the great Mother—the divine Mother—whom the ancients worshipped as the giver of life, has in her care or under her direction the great angels who serve humanity.

It seems to be a part of our thanksgiving service that we should open our consciousness to these angel beings—these beings who have in their care and under their direction the countless tiny nature spirits who work on the earth, work to build up the life-force in the ground, in the flowers, in the fruit, in the trees; in all nature. These tiny nature spirits, who are directed by the winged beings—those whom we call angels—are held as it were in groups in the mind of these superior beings, and they work under their direction. Now, these little nature spirits, who work so beautifully amongst the flowers in the earth, in a sense surrender their own will to a higher will. They work in groups, in companies. And they work with harmony and with great joy. And they must be rewarded when they see joy in the lovely fruits of the earth which their work and their service has helped to bring forth.

We are only conscious of the human world. We have got to expand. We are very small and very narrow-minded. We have got to get beyond this narrow little field of human consciousness, and we have got to realize that there are other fields of consciousness, just as beautiful. Indeed, far more beautiful than the human life and the human consciousness.

Now, we are here in this physical body to do this very thing. To open, to expand our consciousness into these other fields of life.

Minesta was sure that her awareness of the angelic and fairy life behind physical form sprang from a previous life when such knowledge had been part of the wisdom of the whole community. She wrote on another occasion:

✍ Our thoughts just now are of the golden harvest. One of my earliest and happiest recollections is of a field of waving golden corn, swaying in the gentle summer breeze. As a child I remember how thrilled and delighted I was to be taken from London to a Sussex village by the sea for the annual summer holiday. I remember so vividly waking up, very excited, and from my bed looking through the window to a field of golden corn and imagining it bowing to me and saying, 'Good morning, good morning.' To me this was quite a magical moment, for I thought I saw laughing, dancing fairies playing in the field, and enticing me to join them in the fun. What a memory! In following springtimes I used to count the weeks and days, ticking them off on the calendar until it came to the end of July, because then the loveliest time of all arrived—holidays and the golden harvest.

For a child so much happiness can come through the association of ideas, and I wonder what is the memory that has engrained the vision of sowing and reaping so deeply in my soul? Over the years I have become sure that there is a memory going back to Mayan days; a memory of a ritual when the golden grain was scattered into the brown earth and our communal gathering when we as children joined with our elders in the chanting of a mantram, calling upon the hosts of etheric beings from those we would now call fairies, gnomes, and sylphs, to their commanding angels, to gather the forces of the White Light to fertilize and stimulate the growth of the seeds of the previous harvest. This memory has sometimes been as vivid to me as the childhood recollections of this incarnation, when I saw the fairy folk in the corn and recognized their kinship with me as they bade, 'Good morning, good morning, come and join us in our work and play!'

To many, in these modern days, these words may strike an incongruous note. But those of us who have a clear vision of etheric worlds know that without the cooperation of the nature or angelic forces, there would be no harvest. We associate harvest time with the great Mother, who is the provider, through the magical process of growth in the warm brown earth, of the food without which life on the physical plane could neither be developed nor sustained.

The date of the traditional festival of St Michael and All Angels, 29th September, was also the date of the opening and dedication of New Lands, the country home for White Eagle's work which was established in 1945. Minesta felt a great significance behind this sometimes-forgotten festival and she wrote of this and of her conception of the figure of St Michael in an article in the Lodge magazine.

✐ September 29th is the feast of St Michael and All Angels. Little appears to be known in these days about the significance of these inner festivals; and indeed most people regard the celebration of such an event with doubt, if not with cynicism.

What is an angel? The dictionary says: 'A divine messenger, a ministering spirit; a guardian or attendant spirit; a lovely or innocent being entertained unawares; an old

English gold coin, called a noble, showing Michael piercing the dragon of evil.' This will serve to show how deeply recognition of angels has been graven into our race-consciousness.

If there is no reality in angels, then what is the origin of the many legends and stories about the visitation of angels to earthly men and women? In the Bible are many records of the visitation of angels or divine messengers, as when the angel came to the Apostle Peter in prison to unloose his chains, and to throw open the locked and barred doors for his release. Sometimes the descriptions resemble those of ordinary human beings, but in many cases the divine messenger is portrayed with wings.

The writer remembers visiting Hereford Cathedral one day shortly after the celebration of the Holy Eucharist, and was overwhelmed to see on either side of the altar a glorious and winged angel. The angelic forms seen were most beautiful; the faces shone with the light of heaven, and there appeared to be 'wings', or what under closer inspection proved to be elliptical 'sweeps' of light issuing from the shoulders of the divine messengers. The answer, therefore, to the natural question as to whether angels really have wings is that these are not feathered growths from the shoulders, but swirls of divine light in the aura which appear like huge wings.

It is always difficult to comprehend or visualize beings such as angels, who are far above and beyond man in spiritual evolution. Nevertheless, angels are real beings, more real than man, for the reason that the body of man is temporal and passes away, leaving behind the divine spirit which is eternal; but angels are creatures without the coarse physical body, and are therefore all spirit. The great and the heavenly angels live and function in a world of pure spirit, and their bodies are composed of a finer, more subtle and beautiful ether than any substance that we on earth can conceive. There are many degrees of angels, from the highest and chief called St Michael, down to the tiny fairies and nature spirits who may occasionally become familiar playmates to children in garden or countryside. Several books on the subject of fairies and angels give interesting facts about these extraordinarily beautiful creatures.

The high and holy angels at the apex of this evolutionary line of nature forces are truly divine agents and messengers to earth, their purpose being to help man upward towards his goal of Christhood. If only man would be less sceptical about these beautiful beings who guide and guard him, he could receive a great deal more comfort, satisfaction and inspiration during his mortal life.

There are, moreover, ceremonial angels—that is, angels who are present when ritual is taking place. Their work is to use the emanation produced by the *sincere* invocations and aspirations of those taking part in ceremonial; and with it to construct in the spirit world forms of great beauty through which the divine life-forces can work for the beautification of man's life. There are also angels of music; creative angels of all beautiful art; angels of consolation; angels of joy and happiness; and the latter are very lovely to watch as they gracefully dance and play with wondrous coloured streams of spiritual force—much as the angels of music can take the emanations of colour which proceed from a fine orchestra, and rising higher and higher above the earth weave the colours into radiant gossamer forms of buildings and temples which are used and enjoyed by people in the spirit life.

There are also special angels to guard and preside over countries and races. There is a tradition that the archangel St Michael is the guardian angel of our own land, and without wishing to limit this great being I have felt this inwardly to be true. This wonderful being is seen to be clothed in garments like shining and shimmering gold, and holds in his right hand a sword of flashing light. His hair is golden as sunlight; his face with its perfect features shines with a heavenly light. Surrounding his head is a halo of rays; he is enveloped in an aura of soft pulsating rainbow colours through which shine the flashing rays of a great Sun; for he is in truth a Sun-spirit, a Sun-god, the chief of all heaven's angels; who work under his command labouring to overcome ignorance, and to help mankind on its upward and homeward journey to the centre or heart of all good—God.

The feast of St Michael and All Angels—of Michaelmas—on September 29th is a time when those on earth can receive beautiful vision and undoubted blessings, if through sincere prayer they raise their consciousness to the angelic spheres of life, and there await the inflow of the streams of divine love. These, through the work of St Michael 'and all angels', are poured out to stimulate and strengthen the growth of goodness and love, and to hasten the day when all good shall prevail on earth; when man shall live at last in the realization of his at-one-ment with *all* life—in the heart of God.

There is a link between the saint Michael and the legendary King Arthur of Britain.

The light of the spiritual Sun is here, buried in Britain; and it waits for the people of this island to awaken to an understanding of its significance, and to the reality of the presence of the invisible Brotherhood of the White Light. From this Brotherhood they can receive spiritual guidance and protection.

Once on a visit to Tintagel, the legendary birthplace of King Arthur, the writer found an extraordinary spiritual power. It came from the presence of angels; and leading them like a great warrior could be seen the glorious form of the saint Michael, riding a white horse and brandishing his sword of spiritual light.

At Tintagel I lay, with my eyes closed, within the enclosure of the old castle on the grass above the cliff; and the Shining Ones were all around urging the people to accept the Sword of St Michael—which is the sword of truth, the sword of the spirit. It is a symbol of the enormous power which can come to man when at last he understands how to use the Christ light which is in his innermost heart. It can bring to man supreme mastery over his physical body and earthly life. It is the imprisoned splendour in man, the hidden mystery and the secret of God-life. St Michael is the leader of all the angels in heaven, whose influence impresses the earth from time to time when he has a particular mission—such as to herald the ushering of a new age, or when there is a battle to be won over the powers of evil.

This being who has never incarnated on earth directs his pure spiritual influence through the symbolic figures of King Arthur and also St George. This fact should give the British people cause to take serious thought concerning their present spiritual opportunity; which is to play a larger part in bringing into the world knowledge and understanding of man's true nature; and to set a standard of religious freedom and spiritual unfoldment of the Christ within humanity. This is the only, the fundamental basis for reform of all kinds. This is what is meant by the appearance of St Michael riding across the world on his white horse, brandishing his shining sword of the Christ-spirit. His is a cleansing influence and prepares the way, behind the scenes of earthly life, for the second coming of the Saviour, the arisen Christ within man's own heart.

On another occasion much later in life she wrote of a flash of vision that had come to her in the early hours of the morning, around the time of the spring equinox. These are her words:

✍ A deep and heavenly peace enfolded me. I was impressed with the eternal creative life, the white light which I can see clairvoyantly is stirring in all nature, and which is also the connecting line in the silent communion of spirit with spirit in humanity. The symbolic form of the divine Mother slowly appeared, as a mother about to give birth to a child; I heard music like an orchestra tuning up in preparation for this miracle of birth. Then the music vibrated throughout the nature kingdom and I saw a heavenly company of angels, fairies and nature spirits in the white ether, coming close to the earth plane to assist in the spring equinox. A deep silence and stillness enfolded me, a hushed expectancy.

This same miracle takes place within humanity as well as in nature. There are times in every human life when this beauty and wonder comes, when we know deep within us that beauty is truth and that this truth is love. Slowly in our lives, as in nature, the expectancy becomes the reality.

This glimpse of the activity on the inner planes behind the bursting forth into leaf and growth of nature perhaps puts into words for us the source of the gentle exhilaration we can all feel with the coming of spring.

In this opening of vision she was aware of the form and influence of a Mother spirit, or the symbolic form of divine Mother. In her contact with the inner life the influence and the presence of divine Mother were very real to her. Indeed this awareness formed one of the keynotes of her work. Even at an outer level she so often had the gift and the impulse to be creating a home—first of all for her family such as the home the shy, but inwardly strong, London girl created in the Australian bush; but later in life, as her work unfolded, she was deeply conscious of wanting to create a home—many homes—for White Eagle's work. She wanted those who were taking part in White Eagle's work to feel as if they were coming to a home where there was the feeling of the safety, the reassurance of love, in which a heart naturally opens. Behind the physical building and furnishing of a home was the particular feeling of building a form—a home—at an inner level; and the importance of stressing the aspect of divine Mother at a time when deeply ingrained in the thoughts of so many people in the Christian world was the image of God as the Father. We are sure too that there was a deep purpose in White Eagle's use of a woman as his instrument, which was to enable him in his teaching to make real—not just offer at a theoretical level—what he once called, with quiet understatement, 'the gentle divine Mother influence of which we are so fond'.

Amongst Minesta's unpublished writings there is perhaps no one passagewhich does full justice to how strong an emphasis this was in her life, but it may be that something of it is conveyed by the following piece of writing, which was originally entitled 'The Great Mother'.

✎ I was asked the other day why the colour gold seems to prevail in the spring, and the immediate answer that came was 'because yellow or gold is the predominating colour of the sun, the life-giver'. At the call of the sun, life springs from the brown earth after its long winter rest and once again all nature demonstrates the ancient truth that there is no death.

At this time of recurring life one remembers the provision mother earth makes for her children. Nature is the great Mother, the giver of life and the provider and sustainer of that physical form which is the clothing of the spirit. Mankind is apt to accept all nature's gifts as a matter of course: the sun rises in the morning and sets at night, the law of gravity draws down the water of life from the clouds, filling the seas, rivers, lakes and brooks, and giving needed moisture to the earth, helping seeds to germinate and flowers to grow. All this wonder is so often accepted by man without any thought for the great law behind these happenings.

Man himself is a part of nature and a product of natural law. Whatever he thinks, or however carelessly he lives, he is bound and enfolded within this cosmic law. He cannot escape beyond its bounds, and if he tries to do so he is hurt, or in the words of ancient freemasonry, 'he comes up against a sharp instrument'. If he goes against the laws of nature his health suffers and the body deteriorates. His health, vitality and general well-being depend on his degree of harmony with natural forces, even as humanity's well-being and progress depends on its intelligent response to and cooperation with natural and divine law.

We *are* because God is. We live within the life-forces of our Creator. God the Creator is both Father and Mother to all the human family. God the heavenly Father is holding and directing all the heavenly powers and virtues of the spirit. The ancients worshipped God the Mother because they could see in her the producer of life, and recognized nature as the great earthly Mother, producer of physical form and the grain and fruits to nourish it.

Men and nations reach their greatest splendour by obeying the law of unity between man and nature; but when there is deviation from this law, disintegration and degeneration begins. As we realize our unity with all nature, we are drawn consciously into the protection and love of the great Mother, who is our source of supply for all physical needs.

Thought of in this way, the divine Mother becomes more than Mary the mother of Jesus. According to the teaching of the ancient White Brotherhood, divine Mother is the instrument of the Creator, the second aspect of the trinity, the receptacle of the divine energy or divine spirit. Divine Mother has at her command all the angelic beings and nature spirits and lesser etheric forms of life whose work in nature is to assist in directing the various cosmic streams of life-force. As man endeavours to work in harmony with the laws of nature, he begins to become conscious of the different forces and forms of energy which surround him and can flow to him from nature and the Cosmos to make healthy and enrich his physical form.

Searching among the recorded prayers and invocations which Minesta gave we are again struck with how deeply she felt the need to bring the principle of womanhood to the fore, to restore what she felt inwardly was a lost balance in contemporary life. This chapter ends with a moving invocation given during the course of a meeting in the White Eagle Lodge for the work of radiating the star. Although it takes up just a few lines we are sure it conveys something from the depths of her heart. May it also show something of the depth of conception of the work that she founded and sought to share.

✍ Let us in spirit feel the presence of the Elder Brethren. Let us feel the vibration, the *om . . . om . . . om*, and send forth the blazing light of the eternal star of human and divine brotherhood. O Father–Mother God, let this star of love shine forth in power and glory into the hearts of all women on this earth. May they be raised in dignity, in spiritual knowledge, wisdom and love to the motherhood of the world. We would send forth the light of the star to all women doctors, nurses, teachers, ministers, to women in the services, to women who are sorrowful, lonely and disappointed—to them all we send forth the blazing star of brotherhood, love and inspiration. We behold the holy mother, Mary. We receive her blessing. We behold the star from the mountain-tops shining upon the womanhood of Britain, and of the world. May it rise in dignity and purity and help to restore the equilibrium of the two aspects of life in the world. Amen.

CHAPTER FOUR

Rescue from the Fields of War

THE WORK which White Eagle charged his earthly brethren faithfully to follow during the years of the second world war is described in the book THE STORY OF THE WHITE EAGLE LODGE, and even more evocatively in the book THE WHITE BROTHERHOOD by Ivan Cooke, which was published two months after the outbreak of war in 1939. Brothers of the Lodge and those committed to White Eagle's work were earnestly asked to maintain a radiation of the light, in the form of the Christ Star of peace and brotherhood, at every third hour of each day. More than ever before White Eagle spoke of the vital need to radiate the star during the darkened years of war: 'Think, my brethren, what the effect would be if millions in your country were thus radiating light! Think what the effect would be if men abandoned desire for accumulation, or protection for self, and held fast to one dominating thought of peace and brotherhood to help men to the way of Christ! Will you make this effort? For we tell you that the hosts of heaven are ready and waiting to help man. The spirit of the light of Christ will save mankind and this spirit alone.... We pray that everyone hearing our words will be touched....'

During the course of this work during wartime Minesta was occasionally given clear vision of the 'other side of the coin'—the peaceful, but vast and unremitting work going on in the spiritual spheres of life to dress the wounds of suffering men and women on both sides of life—above all the wounds of those 'flung violently out of mortal life by violence'. These glimpses are perhaps best understood against the background of the work of healing on the inner planes which White Eagle was calling all who wished to cooperate to devote themselves to.

The following passage describes a vision of a hospital at the level of life behind the physical.

✍ During a meeting of the White Eagle Brotherhood, after we had been projecting love and the light to the sad and bereaved, I had this vision—I saw through the veil of death into the life beyond.

I was taken in spirit by White Eagle to the battlefield. I saw the barren desert and many of the grim horrors of war and death. I knew the guns were hammering away and the noise on earth must be terrible, and yet everything on this, the other side of the veil, seemed calm and still and very peaceful. The bodies of mortally wounded and stricken men were lying around, and I saw parties of stretcher bearers and nurses moving towards each. I realized that they were spirit people; their movements were so calm, their work so precise. Not one of the still forms lying on the earth was missed or passed by. This fact impressed itself upon my mind. I watched with awe and wonder the tenderness and care with which the nurses and bearers raised the men and gently placed them on the stretchers. They had not very far to carry them—only a few yards, it seemed, and then they entered what seemed like the grounds of some great hospital.

Then a solid curtain or wall seemed to build up and the sandy desert faded away. We were in a garden as fresh and as fragrant as a rose-garden in the early hours of a June morning. Complete peace enfolded us. There, in the centre of these fragrant gardens and lawns, now stood a white building, built like a Greek temple, its beauty enhanced by the flowering vines and roses which twined themselves up the pillars and framed the windows and porticos. This was the hospital or healing temple to which these men were gently borne.

Many personal friends, relatives and guides of the newly released souls were gathered in this home of the spirit. A room seemed to be set apart and prepared for each of the unconscious men, to which room they were carried. No hospital on earth can compare with the rare beauty of this healing home. In one spacious hall were many alcoves, partitioned off with white pillars between which hung draperies of soft colouring—blue, mauves, rose, greens—indeed every colour in varying shades from the deepest to the palest hue formed the divans or beds upon which the patients were laid. Curtains were drawn between the pillars to screen the sleeping forms, but each alcove was open at one end to the garden; so that when the sleeper awoke a garden blossoming in early summer would be the first picture he would see; and then his own friends or maybe relatives would be able to come to him across the soft green grass.

Perhaps in this wartime glimpse into the life of the spheres beyond the physical plane we can also find inspiration for centres of true healing in the new age, when spiritual understanding, healing and medical science will surely work in partnership to achieve a deeper form of healing than is at present understood.

The next passage records a vivid and moving impression of the helpfulness of a dedicated and loving group projecting the light of the Christ Star.

✍ A very striking thing happened when we sent out the light to those souls flung out of mortal life by violence. I saw a vast plain like a desert. It was very misty and there were many souls groping about in a semi-conscious state. As the brothers united in sending out the light, I saw a sudden brilliant searchlight sweeping right across this desert plain. These souls were all attracted to this beam of light and it swung round and pointed in the direction of a path towards which all of them commenced to move. I saw that it led to a bridge on which was another light and where there were angel presences who pointed the way forward. I saw all these souls crossing the bridge and moving upwards into the light and towards a very pleasant country scene of fields and pastureland. I noticed there were wild flowers and streams and grassy banks. The souls flung themselves down and heaved a sigh of relief to find they were in safe and familiar country. And then I saw Brothers of the Light come to talk and minister to them. This scene came to me in a flash but I am impressed to give it to you because it shows how far the work of the Brotherhood extends and how it helps souls on the other side of life as well as those on this side of life.

The next passage in this section describes a picture Minesta was given—perhaps a symbolic picture—of the Master. The message is of the importance of our belief in a spiritual reality and holding fast to this vision; how just this, in itself, enables those at a higher level of life to serve and help their human brethren. Minesta describes the figure of this illumined Server:

✍ The face is illumined with a gracious light—the light of love and compassion and goodness. He radiates this light for a very long way as he walks the earth.

I am guided to give this message: he does walk the earth and he goes to many places, places which seem to be dark and unfitting to receive him. He visits these places and carries with him his sweetness. I asked how we could help in his work and the answer came: 'Just by believing that what I tell you is true.' It seems a simple answer yet it is very important. This is the great challenge for every one of us, particularly in these war-ridden years. The better self wants to believe in the presence of the Master. We want to believe that he is carrying his light into the dark places and we want to believe that we, in our individual ways, are able to help him in his mission. He says that we help him most by believing in him for this opens wide the door for him to enter the very heart of mankind. Literally we stand at the gate; we hold it open and he goes through, into the heart of mankind. Maybe if we didn't believe in him and in the White Brotherhood in the heavens, the gate of earth would be fast closed and there would be less light, less hope able to flow to mankind.

I see the Master, and with him a grand company of Elder Brethren. There is a true blessing now being given to the world. All who will, including ourselves, can help the world to receive this blessing by our own attitude of mind towards these spiritual truths and by our daily contacts.

CHAPTER FIVE

From Talks and Open Letters

AS WAS NOTED in the first chapter of this book, Minesta was first called upon to speak from a public platform when she was twenty-one. After the founding of the Lodge in 1936, almost all her public talks were given at meetings and services within the Lodge. The following is an extract from a talk given in the London Lodge in the 1960s, shortly before Christmas, and invokes symbols central to White Eagle's teaching. We think it is right to say that Minesta always found speaking in public a challenge, but her power to hold an audience's attention, a gift which White Eagle was able to make use of in *his* work too, can be sensed from this passage.

 Once, when I was asked what the Lodge is all about I found I could only point to the symbol we have in the chapel here. You can all see what it is, a golden rose on the six-pointed star. It was made by one of our brothers, and I was so impressed and happy when I saw it that I said we must put it up in the London Lodge here. I do recommend you to look at that symbol when you come into the Lodge, because a symbol is the language of the spirit. A symbol is very important, and very valuable. And I know that in the spirit world, in the Halls of Learning and in the Halls of Wisdom people are taught by symbols. And that symbol there, that golden rose, is radiating a message. You may not think it is singing to you, or speaking to you, but it is silently giving you a message. We have also there the symbol of the six-pointed star, which is a symbol of a perfect man: a man made perfect. We are far from perfect yet because we are unbalanced. We are not perfectly poised, perfectly balanced between spirit and matter. But we are striving to be. We are aspiring towards that balance. I would like you to look at that symbol when you come here to commune with the spirit, and to worship.

You will remember White Eagle's words in our reading, 'The whole purpose of life down here is that the spirit, your spirit shall shine within earth's darkness': this is the purpose of life, that we shall achieve balance between heaven and earth, that we shall grow in the consciousness of God. And then there shines or blooms from that star of *light* that beautiful flower now named the Golden Rose. The golden rose is the manifestation or the expression of the Christ light.

This is what our work is about in the Lodge. We are endeavouring to become balanced and to become channels through which this light can manifest. We do not want to be carried away into airy-fairy states. We want to be very balanced with our feet on earth and our head in heaven. And we want to have that golden rose opening at the heart, which means that we are always sending out goodwill, love. I think that love is a beautiful word, but very much misunderstood and misused. But we have to remember there are many degrees of love. But I believe that love at any level is good. We can always love and be good.

The rose we have been thinking of is at the heart centre, and it unfolds as the sunshine or the love of God shines in the heart. That is a very wonderful symbol. I think it is comparable to the lotus flower of the East. Many teachers have said that if one becomes aware clairvoyantly of a lotus flower anywhere about the aura of an individual, one knows that that individual has commenced to unfold his spiritual awareness of life outside the confines of physical matter, and the rose is the same.

It is through man's brain that he is able to interpret what he feels and senses, and this is why the training and the development of the mind and the brain are very valuable. So we must not discard that altogether, but we must recognize its purpose, and never forget to be true to the inner feeling. You can even smell beautiful things, the perfume of the spirit.

The following passage is from a talk given in London on the twenty-first anniversary of the Lodge. The 'million penny fund' had been launched two years previously to pay off the debts remaining from the purchase of the freehold of the London premises—as described in THE STORY OF THE WHITE EAGLE LODGE. Her belief in involving everyone in the project in hand is evident. It is a belief and a gift which she still brings to the Lodge work from the other side of life!

✍ A teacher once said to me, 'Learn the lesson of acceptance.' But I have found that this is the lesson which we on the physical plane of life want least of all to learn. There are occasions, however, when you have no alternative but to accept what happens and say, 'Thy way, O Lord; not my will but Thy will be done in my life.' This is not easy but it is what the saints and seers of all ages have learnt—the humble spirit of acceptance.

But sometimes one has to fight. I well remember—many of you here remember it too—when the bomb came and demolished Pembroke Hall, our first Lodge home, during the war. We had not very long opened and become established under White Eagle's guidance, when everything, it seemed, was broken down and much of the hall destroyed.

Many people asked why White Eagle had allowed this to happen? Why did he let his Lodge go? The answer was simple, as we came to realize later. We had outgrown Pembroke Hall, which was nearly due for demolition in any case. When they told me, 'The Lodge has gone!' I said at once, 'Never mind, we will get another.' And we went straight off to the estate agent the next week, and he sent us here. As soon as I entered the building I said, 'Yes, this is it, we shall work here.' The point is this: if we had not been forced to move we should never have found this Lodge standing waiting for us. Do you not think this is a wonderful story?

My heart tonight is just overflowing with thankfulness. With very great joy I tell you something which I know will please you all. This week, one of the old members who was with us at Pembroke Hall—she is here tonight—gave me a gift which completed the first Million Penny Fund.

So we have arrived at our target of one million pennies! Is not that wonderful news? In less than two years this has happened. It was White Eagle's inspiration that made me launch the Million Penny Fund. We felt that people could spare a few pennies when they could not spare pounds, so it was a task in which everyone could share. They have indeed done so. These pennies have come from far and wide, and we have been blessed by the love of many people all over the world. Because of this, the Lodge is now practically free from debt.

We should also be deeply grateful and thankful for all the help and guidance given to us by White Eagle and those on the other side who are guiding this Lodge; because it is only due to this very detailed guidance that this Lodge has safely weathered twenty-one years. We have done exactly as we were told, however big the problem—and some mighty big problems have come along. We have just had to hold on in faith, and do what we were told. None of us can do more than what we believe is the right and the best thing. If we do our best then, most surely, God, through His ministering angels, will do the rest. The materialist may laugh at this. Yet even materially-minded people sometimes have to admit a miracle. When you come into close touch with bright and pure spirits you begin to realize the power of their love. But they are only ministers—it is really the eternal love of our Creator which is everywhere, in everyone. All man has to do is to draw it out of his friends and give it out himself.

One or two suggestions have been made about what we shall do now we have reached our object of the million pennies. Let us realize that we shall never during our lifetime achieve the great object of the Great White Brotherhood above. They have the Plan. We are the builders, and we have to lay our foundation first.

So I have just sent out a thought asking, 'What next, White Eagle?' And the answer comes instantly, 'We want another million pennies, please!' So we have to gird up our loins and to start all over again. But this sort of thing happens many times in life. Having got through one phase, we have to start another. I remember White Eagle saying to this congregation, 'When you finally succeed in climbing the golden peak you will have a wonderful view, for you will see many other and finer peaks waiting for you to climb.' So we cannot stay or rest on our laurels. We must keep on keeping on.

May God bless you. And may God bless His work here in this Lodge. With your love and your cooperation there will be a rich harvest. We ourselves may not live here to the true fullness of it, but we shall see future generations enjoy the fruits of our labours while we are enjoying our release to greater freedom and love.

God bless you all!

We return now to Minesta's written word and to an earlier glimpse of her care for the fabric of White Eagle's work—an awareness that the real fabric of this work of the spirit was not buildings, but human hearts and lives—the growing band of friends of White Eagle which even in the late

1940s spread far beyond the two main centres in England. It was to bring a feeling of closeness and connection in this widely scattered 'family' that Minesta instituted a regular open letter in the then-monthly publication *Angelus*. It was called 'The Chain of Fellowship'. This is the opening of the first letter in September 1949:

✍ Dear Friends,

For a long time I have wanted to write you a personal letter because I have felt the need to establish some form of direct communication between us. This feeling has been inspired through reading many letters from you posted from many countries. We want *Angelus* to fulfil the function of a personal and human link so that we in London can reach out to you who are physically far removed from us.

Some time ago a note was put into *Angelus* asking you to remember the great pressure of work which builds up in the form of correspondence, but I would not like this to cut you off from brotherhood with us in spirit. I read all the letters which come and because I now find it impossible to reply to each one personally I have asked to be allowed to write to you each month in *Angelus*. This means that although only one letter will actually be written I shall endeavour to answer if I can questions asked in your letters. I hope in this way to form a chain, with our ever-increasing family throughout the world as its links. From time to time extracts will be given from the letters received, particularly from our readers living a long distance away, so that there will follow a building-up of this friendly feeling throughout the world, like that which we have endeavoured to establish at the London Lodge and the New Lands home. By this means I hope all our readers will feel they are in personal touch and can also share each others' interests.

You may not know that at 7.00 pm every Monday we meet in the chapel at the London Lodge so that in thought and in spirit as a brotherhood we can project thought-waves of the Christ light out into the world. At this time we link *in thought* with all our members, and with those in contact with White Eagle's teaching through *Angelus*.... So wherever you are, however remote your physical circumstances from the brotherhood in London or at New Lands, remember that at this time particularly, a flash of thought and love links you with the group of human brothers who have worked in this way for many years with the Brotherhood in spirit to make their contribution for the spiritual advancement and well-being of all humanity, and that by this means you can help in their work.

A few months later she returned to the purpose of this new letter and wrote of how, although the work had grown to a size when it was no longer possible for her to maintain outward personal contact with all White Eagle's friends, she knew that those who responded to his teaching were able to make their own link of spirit with him. The terms in which she wrote of this are inspiring and we know still as true today.

✍ My Dear Friends,

Thank you all who have written to me your constructive, appreciative and friendly letters. It is grand to feel the increasing spirit of brotherhood amongst all friends and followers of the White Eagle teaching. Although many of us have never met, I know there is a common meeting ground for us all in the temple of the spirit; for there we are learning to speak the same language and so shall recognize each other whenever and wherever we meet. In sleep and in meditation I have caught a glimpse of a sunlit valley encircled by golden-topped mountains. In that valley a vast assembly gathers in openness and comradeship, waiting for the summons into the various 'halls' of learning and wisdom. Many whom I know enter one of these 'halls' to listen to the gentle words of the one we know as White Eagle. How far his words travel from this spirit temple no-one can estimate, although some idea of the widespread influence of this teaching is coming home to us in the London White Eagle Lodge, when we read with much happiness the many letters from friends at home and abroad.

One friend who writes from Norway speaks of the clarity and simplicity of this teaching. This, I believe, is the keynote of White Eagle's mission on earth—simplicity. He gives profound truth as plainly and clearly as possible. Sometimes his message may seem too simple for those who delight in complex phrases and even occult mysteries; but after all, however advanced you are in occult lore, truth lies within the heart. The Master Jesus chose the simplest language and commonplace illustrations from everyday life to reveal the wisdom of the divine law governing all life.

In the bi-monthly magazine *Stella Polaris*, which succeeded *Angelus* in 1951, the Chain of Fellowship letter continued, always with answers to readers' letters and questions. The following is a response to questions about the character of 'elder brothers' of the spirit.

✍ The manner of the appearance of the White Brethren depends entirely upon the circumstances and the conditions available to their use. I feel impressed to stress here that they are most human, gentle, kind, and very simple and courteous, conveying always a feeling of perfect ease and extraordinary happiness. They make no effort to impress their greatness, but they do, as my Indian friend said, express most wonderful love.

Are the Masters intellectually powerful and of great occult skill?

The Masters naturally possess extremely powerful intellects, but intellect is veiled almost to obscurity by their gentle and tender love and human understanding of our youth, inexperience and frailty. They naturally possess great occult skill which they only exercise for the spiritual advancement of individuals or communities, and never exhibit for self-aggrandizement or to satisfy the curious. Pure white magic, which is the power the White Brethren used in occult work, is only put into operation by the Christ-power which is divine Love; this is slowly, very slowly, developed, through many incarnations, and through self-mastery.

What should we be and how should we live and appear if we became Masters? To what stature of humanity should we have developed? How are we, looking upon ourselves as subjective egos, related to the objective being of the Masters or Adepts?

If and when we become Masters our appearance would be divinely human. I think the Masters when visiting our earthly plane of life exemplify the most natural, pure and perfect ideal; that is to say, man made perfect—with complete mastery over himself and over physical matter. Our relationship to our Masters is that of a tiny brother or sister to the adult. We have far to go, much to learn and many things to conquer in ourselves; and this in all probability will take many, many lives. However, the goal is certain and the ideal of the Christ man is held before us, and is symbolized by the six-pointed star—a life, perfectly balanced with feet on earth, and face uplifted to the spiritual sunlight, self-disciplined and poised, and above all, manifesting all the attributes of Christ.

Here is the answer to a question on clairvoyant vision.

✍ Not all clairvoyants see spirits in the same way. One can liken clairvoyance to any other form of seeing. Do we all see exactly the same beauty in a landscape or a painting? One of the poets said, 'The beauty is in the eye of the beholder.' I would say that the degree of clairvoyance depends upon the nature and capabilities of the reflector, that is to say, the particular chakra which is animated in the medium or seer. For there are a number of levels upon which a sensitive person can see clairvoyantly, much as there are a number of planes on which a spirit can function after death, depending entirely upon the spiritual growth of the person. Therefore I can only answer this question from my own particular and limited experience of clairvoyance. I have seen spirits of ordinary, kindly, human people—perhaps like ourselves—appearing in exactly the same clothes as they wore when on earth—wearing identical dresses, jewellery and clothes, but usually looking younger in facial expression and also illumined; that is, looking as though they had an electric radiance switched on inside them, which makes them appear less dense and earthy and more ethereal or heavenly. When spirits have been in the higher world for a longer time, they entirely lose the earthy look and are more often seen in an aura of light, with the physical form just clothed in soft drapery; and when seen like this they convey a feeling of intense joy, happiness, love and peace.

Characteristic of Minesta's writing in the magazine are seasonal reflections; the first here is on 'Autumn':

✍ To me autumn is deeply satisfying. I used not to feel like this when I was young. In youth one responds to the upsurge of the life-forces, but in maturity one becomes attuned to the harmonies which seem to blend all the varying levels and aspects of life into one, like the many flowers in a bouquet. Even in the withdrawal of the spirit, of life, one recognizes a wonderful truth—for to lay down the physical form gently and graciously after its use is over is all part of the true pattern of life.

When meditating on this, I had a vision of life as an eternal round, as something very beautiful indeed in which each changing season brings its own special gift, its own particular message to the human soul if we will listen. The spirit within us is forever linked with the source of life, our Creator, our beneficent, all-enfolding and loving heavenly Father, and there is no end and no beginning. This thought reminds me of Wordsworth's words:

> Not in entire forgetfulness,
> And not in utter nakedness,

But trailing clouds of glory do we come
From God, who is our home.

When we can reach back to the beginning, the source of life's stream, we shall no longer feel old or saddened by thoughts of leaving our physical body and those whom we love; because as we enter into the stream of life in fuller consciousness, we can find promise and fulfilment in all the rhythm of the seasons. Every end is a beginning. In all our human life we are sowing and reaping in expectation of a golden harvest on earth or in a higher world.

The following passage describes her understanding of the inner meaning of Christmas.

✍ The year has passed and on looking back we can be thankful to the loving and guiding hand of God which has brought us along our earthly and spiritual journey. Much has happened in the world and to you and me during the last year. Sunshine and shadow we have encountered, but as we arrive at another Christmas we can be thankful for a very rich experience which has brought us—or should have brought us—an increase of understanding.

I know that White Eagle would like to help all find real joy in the Christ-Mass. I have noticed how very mixed are people's feelings about Christmas. Some anticipate the season with dread, for it holds poignant memories. To others it brings anxiety, and material burdens because we take hardly the extra work entailed. For the children and the young in heart it is a time of fun and gaiety. The feeling I am given from White Eagle however is to greet the coming of Christmas as a happy, healthy mother will greet the birth of her baby. New birth is for ever a miracle, in a sense an initiation, and to the mother brings an expansion of consciousness. Perhaps this is why ancient races worshipped the mother and child as their God, as ancient monuments testify, for to them motherhood stood as a symbol of the promise of eternal life. Christmas is essentially the time of the Mother. The Christ-spirit is born of the divine Mother-love in the heart of every man, woman and child. Christmas is a time of giving, loving and home-making. It is the Mother who prepares the cradle (the home, or the heart) for the reception of the babe Christ; and oh what joy there is in this preparation, anticipation and final rejoicing when the Child is born!

This mystic spirit can come alive, can be born in the heart of everyone at

Christmastime if self is put out; for then the soul (symbolizing the Mother) prepares itself to receive the lovely new-born Christ babe, which nestles in its cradle, the human heart. Perhaps it is real mothers who can best know the infinite joy of this strange mystic birth—a joy which knows no bounds, which bursts through all apparent material limitation, such as anxieties, cares and sorrows created entirely by earth conditions, and like a bird (the symbol of an initiate) wings its way heavenward in an ecstasy of praise and thanksgiving for life itself. This, the true festival of Christmas, is the birth of the light within the heart-consciousness. Not only one human being but all humanity should celebrate the birth of Christ, the Son of God. This is the recurring birth of new life, of spiritual light which is a love welling up in every heart which beats with life. Whatever our particular burden this Christmas, our secret sorrow, disappointment or fear, may we rise above it and so see it in its true perspective. Then we shall realize how trivial it is, how incomparable with the ecstasy of a Christmas festival which should fill our hearts and our homes, if we endeavour to welcome the mystical birth of the Christ-spirit.

This is what White Eagle wishes for us—the happiness of the communion of Christ-Mass.

Finally, two passages from Chain of Fellowship letters which are perhaps 'shadow' and 'light': the first a consideration of isolation and loneliness, which certainly holds several references to personal experience; the second a mention of perhaps the deepest experience of union in her own life.

✍ Dear Friend,

This is the form of address I like best because everyone needs a friend. Indeed we must all have experienced moments of loneliness and isolation, when we feel acutely the need of spiritual companionship—of someone so attuned to us that the spoken word can be dispensed with; and in the inner quietness of the spirit only the language of the spirit can convey the comfort, the assurance, the strength and the inspiration so much needed at the time.

These moments come to us all, whether or not we admit the fact; and it is not necessarily the death of a dear one that brings to us that sensation of being bereft and isolated from life. Of course what we are really separated from at such moments of despair is *God*. But you will ask, 'How shall we find God when we are in complete darkness, and the "heavens seem as brass"?' Even little children suffer; perhaps it is in childhood that the seeds of indifference are sown—as when the child feels acutely the pain of non-understanding and indifference on the part of its elders. The reaction of the young to their elders' lack of understanding of their emotional needs often lays a foundation for a cynical outlook on life, and a selfishness which is also found at the core of a disintegrated, chaotic society. This spreads far beyond the confines of the personal into our national life and finally into many international relationships....

This all leads one to see how everyone is indeed 'his brother's keeper' and also how responsible we are for the karma of one another, and even of the whole world. We have heard much about personal responsibility without perhaps understanding that it stretches to infinity, and that even our thought has its effect upon other lives. Although we may feel independent and at times suffer the misery of loneliness and isolation, we are nevertheless like grains of sand on the shore of the vast life of spirit, we are like drops in the ocean, and cannot be separated from the other grains of sand or drops of water.

God is all in all; therefore as we are part of God, we too are all in all, and so form part of every other individual speck of life. Our efforts to do good, and to be good as God is good, are efforts towards the perfection of life as a whole. If we inflict pain upon other parts of God's family, we must necessarily feel a similar measure of pain, because to do it to another is really to do it to ourselves. The law of God is broken when man acts other than with love towards his fellow creatures, and our life on earth has to bring us to an understanding of this principle of brotherhood. Whenever we feel desolate and lonely, it would be a comfort to remember that in simple thoughts of love we are no longer separate but united with countless companions of our spirit. We move towards the consciousness of being part of the whole, as we live and strive both for self-consciousness and God-consciousness.

✍ I believe that this Lodge was not brought into being by earthly will or power; nor has it been maintained by the comparatively feeble efforts of earthly people, who may not hold clearly the true vision we are given; but its existence is due primarily to the power and the help which has continually been given from above.

What material proof can we give to a world which laughs at such an idea? Well, again the only proof is what one receives oneself within one's own being. Such proof is absolutely unshakeable to the person concerned. The same applies to experiences with the life beyond. I myself once had an experience many years ago—quite suddenly. I was sitting down doing some sewing. All of a sudden my consciousness of this earthly plane went. I was right away into a condition of life which can only be described as universal or cosmic. A flash of blazing heavenly light swept me up into its heart, and I seemed to belong everywhere, to be part of every living breathing particle of existence. I belonged to all the past and all the future. In this brief ecstasy, I realized eternity and infinity. When I returned to my confined earthly consciousness the only words that would serve to express what I, in my inner soul then knew, were simply, 'There is no death.' There would never be such a thing as death because we were all eternal in our cosmic life. Now, that is an experience which comes to the human soul perhaps only once, and when it comes and the consciousness is thus raised, it does not matter whether millions of people laugh. The soul knows forever that this is truth and that there is no death—that one is attached eternally to some life of the spirit which is gloriously happy, which has fulfilment, which holds everything for us that our hearts have ever longed for. In such realization you are at one with universal life.

We are down here in this physical body, struggling with all the difficulties and problems but not just for fun—but to enable us continually to grow in our spiritual life and power until we all know most surely that there is no death, and that all life is ever unfolding into growth and beauty. That is our mission here.

CHAPTER SIX

Glimpses of the Temple

MINESTA'S greatest vision was expressed, not in words, but in bricks and mortar—the building of the White Temple, 'the Temple on the hill', as White Eagle spoke of it. The building was completed in her eighty-second year. Shortly before the opening White Eagle remarked, 'It has taken a lifetime to get into the minds of our children here the idea, the conception, to build this Temple'—it was surely the final flowering of her life of vision. As is so often the case with spiritual work which represents a great step forward into a new phase of life, the actual building of the temple was not achieved without its share of difficulty, delay and patient resolution of problems. Over three years were to pass between the breaking of the first sod and the final, exultant day of the opening of the Temple in 1974 on 9th June, St Columba's Day. Part of Minesta's work during these years was to keep before everyone's eyes the vision of the Temple and its purpose. One of the ways she did this was through her Chain of Fellowship letter which began each issue of the magazine *Stella Polaris*. The following series of brief extracts from these letters show something of her vision of this first 'White Temple on the hill, at New Lands'.

A Vision (June 1966)

✍ A vision has been given to me by the White Brotherhood behind the veil, of a white temple on the hill at New Lands where the future work of the White Eagle and the Brotherhood in spirit can grow in beautiful and natural surroundings. It will be a place where people can retreat from the material world to study, meditate and develop understanding of the spirit, and learn in their own way to live together in harmony according to the law of brotherhood. The vision was unfolded to me of a community, similar in practice to the earliest Christian brotherhoods.

This brotherhood would be practised by the earthly brethren working in harmony with the nature kingdom, and helped by those beyond the veil. The brethren would learn how, through meditation, to come into touch with the supreme Light and receive knowledge and wisdom from the spirit life which would bring happiness and well-being to man. They would learn to receive strength from God and how to live in the physical life in harmony and peace, and eventually to realize the culminating spiritual healing at the transition of the soul from the physical life to the spiritual—thus all fear of death would be overcome.... I am so impressed with this vision that I am certain that the White Brotherhood in spirit are kindling a flame which will in time burst forth.

A Receptacle for Light (February 1971)

✍ I hope that you will all understand the ideal which White Eagle has placed before us— to build here on the hilltop at New Lands the beautiful White Temple where this power, truth and beauty of the Christ light will centre. I am impressed by White Eagle that in the remote past his people, the ancient Indians, built their stone temples not so much for ritual but as *receptacles* for the Christ-power. Ceremonies performed within these temples were done with knowledge and understanding of how such ceremonies worked on the invisible planes to build up a concentration of the Great White Light for the blessing of the earth. I hope that all our readers who have been so kind and generous in their support of this project, will get a clear vision of what White Eagle is endeavouring to do in this, his building of the White Temple.

Many Hands, Many Thoughts (August 1971)

✍ Sometimes when such a project as this is launched, a few major gifts serve to provide all the funds required, but in the case of our White Temple, the money is being raised by a very large number of small amounts: so this really will be a temple built by the human effort and the hearts and spirit of White Eagle's family.

Foundations ... and Bricks (October 1972)

✍ When these words are read holidays will be over for most of us; summer will have passed and we shall be approaching the fall of the year with thanksgiving for the many gifts both physical and spiritual which life has brought to us during our summer days. So often it is the small, almost unnoticed things that bring continuing happiness, and so we shall search our hearts to recall events which have brought to us a deeper peace, a natural joy, and helped us to realize the treasure to be found in our innermost being.

As a contrast, try to assess the difference it might make to you if you knew nothing whatever about the spirit life of man. I think it would be like living imprisoned in a small, dark, windowless room, with no view of the glorious panorama of life which White Eagle and the White Brotherhood work to present to us.

No doubt you will be anxious to know how the Temple building is progressing. Work, which started in May, went ahead very briskly indeed at first, so that in the first stage a very solid, strong foundation was laid, which included insulation to conserve the warmth from the under-floor heating; and the foundations for the twelve pillars to support the upper structure and domed roof. Then ensued a *very* long wait for a promised consignment of special white bricks for the outer walls! The majority of bricks and other materials have now been delivered and it will be possible for the building to be restarted any day now.

We who are living here on the spot can daily watch the lovely White Temple coming into manifestation, which the White Brotherhood in spirit have inspired, and which, in cooperation with our many earthly friends, the human instruments, they are building on this hillside at New Lands. I hope you will be pleased with the completed structure, the work of a fine architect who is carrying out White Eagle's wishes. Our architect told me that he was first inspired in his picture of the Temple by thoughts of Stonehenge, one of the oldest sun temples known in Britain.

The deeper we go into White Eagle's philosophy, the clearer it becomes to us that it is all based on the worship of the Sun, or Son, of God, and on the life of the Son on earth—the Christ-spirit manifesting in mankind.

The Shell Complete (August 1973)

✍ I know you will be very happy to learn that, after many months of delay and the overcoming of many obstacles, the 'shell'—that is to say, the walls and all the roof excepting the dome—of the lovely White Temple is on the point of completion. It stands out, high on the hill, visible over a wide area. Many of our friends have remarked on the pure spiritual power which can be felt there, and have seen the light radiating far and wide. White Eagle said, in September 1971: '...even when [the Temple] is only a shell, when you go into it you will feel the everlasting arms are around you', and this is true.

I awoke recently with a vivid picture in my mind of the Temple shining white like a beacon light amid the fresh green of the countryside. White Eagle was very close to me, reminding me that the real architects and builders of our Temple—or their inspirers—are the builders of the ancient sun temples to be found all over the world....

For many years devoted brethren have gathered in groups at certain magical hours, mentally and spiritually to send out this light of spiritual healing, both to individuals and whole nations. By their work perhaps unconsciously they have helped to build the spiritual temple soon to become a reality on the physical plane of life. It is a Temple which is being built by a great chain of spiritual devotion across the world.

Standing Beneath the Open Sky (October 1973)

✍ This letter is being written on 2nd August, and you will be reading it sometime during October or possibly November, so you will understand how difficult it is to give you up-to-date news of the White Temple on the hill here at New Lands. At the time of writing I have just returned, uplifted, from my daily visit to it. Already the power is building up there, and as I stood in the centre of this enfolding structure, looking up through the open circle (which awaits the domed roof) to the heavenly blue sky, I was deeply aware of an encircling company. I saw the Temple again as an immense Grail Cup, a receptacle for the Christ love, the Christ light. I feel impressed to pass this vision on to you, so that you too will keep it in mind and meditate upon its meaning. This Temple, built on earth by the kindness and generous help of many, many friends and co-workers with White Eagle, and on the inner plane by their worship, and loving, devoted service, will in the future become one of the centres of the White Light in this country....

I have just received from one of our members on holiday on Iona a beautiful picture of St Columba's 'blessed isle'. It is just on forty years since we first went there, and I shall never forget it. As we crossed the sea and drew nearer to Iona it seemed to me that we were drawing near to an island of light; for although the day was not particularly sunny, from all around there arose a very clear white light. After that occasion we spent many holidays on Iona, revelling in the unbelievably lovely colours of the island and the surrounding sea, and we all felt we were drawing strength and blessed peace from the spiritual power centred there. I mention this because I think it illustrates a point I have been trying to make, that these communities or brotherhoods of former times, or of whatever outward religious persuasion, established by their lives a centre of light, which remains long after they themselves have gone. Everyone who has visited Iona has found it to be a place of special spiritual loveliness. This is the ideal for which we work in the White Eagle Lodge; namely, by worship of the Great White Spirit, by service, and by our life together as a community, to establish a centre of light which will live and radiate its healing blessing long after we are gone. White Eagle wants me to conclude this letter with the words: 'Peace and love be forever with you.'

A Thought on Entering the Temple (April 1974)

✎ White Eagle wants us to realize ever more deeply that thought is all-powerful in life. We are what our thoughts make us, we go where our thoughts take us. All action is the manifestation of thought; all creation is the manifestation of thought. As our spirit home is a creation of our thought, so too our earthly surroundings are dependent not so much on our circumstances but on our thought, for we can surround ourselves with beauty and harmony as an expression of ourselves. This beauty, although it may be unseen, can nevertheless be felt and sensed by those who enter into it. We have had a striking example of this in the building of the Temple. The spirit of all our contributors to the fabric of the new White Temple at New Lands has been built into it—and can clearly be felt as we enter it.... The beautiful White Temple here at New Lands which you have all helped to build is a monument to the faithful company of White Eagle's human friends on earth who are reflecting the light, the power and the love of the Great Spirit above.

Harvest (August 1974)

✎ This year of 1974 we of White Eagle's family have every reason to recognize the beauty of a wondrous harvest, the first seeds of which were sown who knows how many years ago, which is coming to the Lodge in the completion of the White Temple at New Lands. With joy in our hearts we express our deep thankfulness to the Great White Spirit, to the angelic forces and to our dear earthly brethren who have cooperated with them and with us to make this possible. By the time you read these words the Temple will have been dedicated....

CHAPTER SEVEN

White Eagle's Instrument

WHITE EAGLE only rarely spoke about himself and then quite often in passing, as he had no wish to draw attention to himself as a personality. He spoke of himself as being a spokesman; an instrument for a greater brotherhood. Not very often either did he speak about his own relation to his earthly instrument, although this is described by Minesta in her book THE ILLUMINED ONES. However, in one talk given by White Eagle in the early years of their work together, he speaks very simply of the special character of his work and also about his control of his human 'instrument'. This simple teaching gives us a privileged glimpse into the delicacy and refinement of his work with Minesta. Perhaps, also, it gives us a glimpse of the sensitivity required in fulfilling her undertaking to be the 'bridge' across which he could walk half-way to bring his inspiration of brotherhood to so many.

WE COME TO HELP YOU

We pray that the power of God, the eternal spirit of love and wisdom, may be with us. May we be receptive to the light, so that at the close of our communion we may feel that it has been good to have been here. Amen.

May our prayer be truly answered! For as you have heard us say so often, it is not the spoken words so much as the spirit behind them, which, received into the heart, brings a permanent raising of consciousness.

Some years ago, one of our beloved earth children asked us why we come back as we do when we could be away in the heaven world. We answered that we come back, not because we choose the earthly vibration in preference to the heavenly, but because we love you, our earthly brethren; and also because it is a path of service we chose many centuries ago. We chose to come back to earth to help keep the contact between the ancient days and their wisdom, and present-day humanity, between heaven and earth. Do you realize how important is this personal contact between the world of spirit and man on earth? So many people think that man is sufficient unto himself and that he can pursue his path almost unaided; that his own reason, intellect and intuition are sufficient. And also that what happened thousands of years ago is of no concern to men today. But how mistaken is this idea! The personal contact between spirit and man on earth is all important in helping humanity to evolve. Men, made in God's own image, the image of the divine Son, are not separate from one another nor are they separate from God. And brethren from the higher spheres come to help you to hold true spiritual communion with the divine personality.

There are those, too, who think that only the lowest disembodied spirits can communicate. We would explain that highly strung and over-nervous persons are readily responsive to the sphere nearest to the earth; and for them it is sometimes easier to contact what are sometimes described as earthbound spirits, because they are little removed from the vibrations of earth. But it is incorrect to say that *only* these spirits contact earth. God never leaves man without a witness of His love and truth, and there are schools or temples of learning and wisdom in the higher spheres from which, throughout the ages, teachers have descended to earth to bring the light of ancient wisdom to humanity. These teachers have great love and sympathy for earth's humanity, and bring their help in various ways. They do not necessarily control a medium to give spiritual teaching, although this will become more frequent. They may influence or use the instrumentality of certain religious teachers or scientists, or those at the head of important movements likely to affect the thought and outlook of humanity. Behind all these will be found one of these teachers from the temple of wisdom, although these leaders of movements may deny all contact with the super-physical world. The spiritual teacher and inspirer labours on, often unknown by the one on earth, whose lower mind may be closed against truth, but whose higher mind remains unconsciously open. The higher mind can be consciously lifted to the light; or it can remain unconsciously open, even while materialism darkens the lower or outer mind. The teachers of the Ancient Wisdom guide us who come back to serve humanity in the way best suited to humanity's need, at the particular age in which we come.

When we come back to speak to our beloved children, we bring great love to you. You say you can feel the love—well dear ones, it is your own love that you feel! We are so happy in your love. If you went to a friend's house, and your friend opened the door and said, 'Come in, we are so delighted to see you!' you would be happy. But if they peeped through the window and said, 'I do not want you here, go away!' you would feel sad indeed. You may have come laden with fruit and flowers and the gift of love, and then be rejected. Therefore it is a joy to us to find an open door, and loving words and greetings.

A question was once asked as to whether the personality speaking was separate from the instrument used; or was White Eagle the higher aspect, the higher self of the medium. We answer that we are *not* the same personality as this instrument. We are not even a higher aspect of her personality, although we do use her higher self to communicate with you. We use her higher mind, which is in appearance like a globe of pale gold light. In this work you can help us, for we cannot always sustain our hold upon this light ourselves. Disturbing thoughts or even trifling noises can shatter the fine contact we are making. A minute noise can sound like a crash in our midst, and then it is as if the bubble bursts, which takes time to rebuild.

Usually we do not come alone. As we speak to you now, for instance, there are two other brothers present, holding the line of communication; whilst White Eagle, a separate entity from the medium and from the others, speaks to you. You do not question when you hear the announcer on your radio say 'so and so will speak to you'; it never occurs to you to doubt or to suggest that the voice you are hearing is the higher personality of the announcer. The microphone is a material instrument; the higher mind of a medium is a very delicate and subtle spiritual one. As the announcer speaks into a microphone, so we 'speak' into this light, but not in quite the way we are speaking to you now. Thoughts we would convey are projected into the 'microphone' of the higher mind. We control the speech from the pituitary gland, and certain parts of the brain. For want of a better word we say that we 'hypnotize', or know how to influence, certain parts of the brain, which in turn influence the organs of speech.

We are the spokesman for a group; sometimes there are other brothers who come to convey certain truth. Then White Eagle holds the control while the thought, the teaching or truth, comes perhaps from another of our brothers, though we are not separate from one another. If you think of spirit as an ocean, composed of millions of drops, then you may recognize the interpenetration or the one-ness of individual drops in the ocean. Whilst the child I am using is a separate drop, and I, White Eagle, am a separate drop, yet we are as one. Nevertheless there is an age-long bond between us.

We have been asked concerning previous incarnations. It matters very little. We do not want your mind to be bound by any set ideas. People set so much store by a past incarnation, but the personality which manifested is unimportant surely? Only the contribution of that personality to the general good of life, or what was absorbed of the eternal wisdom of God matters.

But since there are questions still.... We have had a number of incarnations in America, both North and South. The personality or the garment we used to find most congenial to resume when contacting the earth was that of a North American Indian. There are many other personalities of course, including one which you know equally well, whom also you call 'White Eagle', and who lived in Central America and again in

Peru. We bring back in certain teaching some of the ancient religion of those days.

One of the principles of the North American Indian religion was the worship and adoration of the divine personalities or gods. In modern life, the ideal of that personal love and understanding of the wise 'gods' or great ones seems to have been lost, and the western world thinks in terms of impersonality. You will see in many countries in the West the idea of a universal and impersonal first Principle, unconcerned with the heart and feelings and emotions of His creature, man. We would lead men back to the all-wise, all-loving and compassionate Father–Mother God, and to the Son of God, the perfect man—perfect in outward form, perfect in his love and sympathy, and in his desire to come to the side of every man and woman and child who calls to him. Let us return to the warmth and compassion and intimacy and loveliness of true communion with the great brother, Christ, Son of a loving Parent.

We are striving to make this truth simple and real to all souls who are guided or drawn to the White Eagle Lodge. We believe this to be the first principle of life, the foundation upon which all knowledge, all intelligence, all expansion of consciousness is built. Although it may sound simple, even childish, to some minds, nevertheless there are those who feel the fundamental need, and they will work with the White Brotherhood—not necessarily by physical labour, but by giving their hearts and love to further the Brotherhood's work.

We come to earth to work in preparation for the second coming of Christ, of the Christ-spirit, that ideal of perfected humanity which lies in the mind of our Father–Mother God.

We would assure our beloved family that we are with them all in spirit; we are by their side, and our only concern is their spiritual growth and expansion of consciousness. We want to make all who are sad, happy; to give them love and make them feel they are needed and have got something for which to work and look forward to. We want all our beloved family to feel that we are *real* brothers with time to consider their troubles and problems. No-one is overlooked, for when the threads of spiritual contact are formed, they never break.

CHAPTER EIGHT

A Window on Eternity

MINESTA herself passed into the world of light on 3rd September 1979, after two difficult and painful years which were surely as much a part of her life's purpose as the rest of her experience. This small book, as stated in the introduction, is in the nature of a special birthday celebration, and we think there is no better way of leaving the book with the sense of a birthday tribute than by sharing a contact made in meditation by her daughter, Ylana Hayward, with Minesta as she now is. We have looked back with thankfulness, but no-one more than Minesta herself would wish our vision to rest on the present, and on the future, our eyes alight with trust and hope.

A little while ago we had, in meditation, an experience which we would like to share with you if we may. After that first still contact which we make in the heart of the star, we knew we had to 'come down' a little into what White Eagle calls the infinite and eternal garden.

We were taken to Minesta's home in that garden. The picture was very clear indeed, and almost as real as the room in which we are sitting to write this letter to you. We were taken into what appeared to be her study, and there was a desk there, at an angle half facing towards the window, and we could see her sitting at the desk, writing and we think studying. We mentally asked, why, in that heavenly state of life when communication, in any case, is by thought, would she need to sit and write? The answer came very quickly, and with her usual wise twinkle, that she still enjoyed putting her thoughts into words in writing! But it was more than that really for we knew, as we looked, that we too could come and sit at that desk when we were wanting to communicate with any one of her White Eagle family and to help them, and that she

would be with us and, in so far as we allowed, speak to you in this way.

But what most impressed us about the room was that one whole side was in the form of a big picture window. As we looked out of the window we found that we were looking onto a view of the White Temple, just across a valley and shining in the sunlight, though there was just a little haze about it which together with the intervening valley conveyed to my mind that it was on a different level of life. Such a beautiful view Minesta had from her home in the spirit world, through the picture window, and we enjoyed it with her. But as we looked we began to wonder, and we asked why, beautiful as it was, she could possibly want to sit looking at the Temple—especially as no doubt she could visit whenever she wished to do so. Then, for a moment, we were in her heart, feeling her love for each one of her 'family' all over the world, and we knew that because the Temple was the heart of the work it was through the Temple that she felt and held in her own heart the need of each one of the family. She was very anxious not to give the impression of being anything wonderful or super-human. Just a mother who still cared very much for her family; and it was as though those who were in need of that mother comfort and guidance could come in spirit to the Temple (which is in heaven as well as on earth) and she would help as she used to do when on earth.

She was also very aware of everything that goes on in the Temple and at New Lands, holding it all in her heart and gently guiding it in the right direction when necessary. And then we could see how through the Temple the link was made with each Lodge—first the old home, the London Lodge, seemed to come gently into focus and she held that in her heart and then the other Lodges and Groups and the Centres overseas and the leaders and workers came into view as the need arose—but always this beautiful view of the Temple shining in the sunlight. She told us once again how close the two worlds are and how she and Brother Faithful come and walk in the Temple and New Lands garden as they used to do and greet and welcome their friends in this garden of reunion. We talked together a little and then the time came for us to withdraw and return to the earth consciousness, which we did very reluctantly. But the picture of Minesta's home and that beautiful room with the view of the Temple through the picture window remains and will always remain a vivid memory.

We have found it difficult to find adequate words to describe the experience but we hope that it may have conveyed a picture which gives her message too.

*

AU REVOIR

We finish with a few words from what turned out to be White Eagle's last message through Minesta to healers within the Lodge:

Build your own bridge, and live with God, and the blessing of the Great White Spirit is with you all.

We will not say 'good-night', nor 'good-bye'. We will say 'God be with you always, as we shall be with you always.'